Sharawadji

For Janet
with best wishes

Brian

28/04/12

Richmond Hill

Sharawadji
Brian Henderson

Brick Books

Library and Archives Canada Cataloguing in Publication

Henderson, Brian, 1948-
    Sharawadji / Brian Henderson.

Poems.
ISBN 978-1-926829-69-2

    I. Title.

PS8565.E51S48 2010   C811'.54   C2010-907675-3

We acknowledge the Canada Council for the Arts, the Government of
Canada through the Canada Book Fund, and the Ontario Arts Council
for their support of our publishing program.

 Canada Council   Conseil des Arts
for the Arts   du Canada   Canadä    ONTARIO ARTS COUNCIL
CONSEIL DES ARTS DE L'ONTARIO

The cover image is a photograph by Brian Henderson.

The book is set in Minion and FF DIN.

Design and layout by Alan Siu.
Printed and bound by Sunville Printco Inc.

Brick Books
431 Boler Road, Box 20081
London, Ontario N6K 4G6

www.brickbooks.ca

For Charlene, for ever

Contents

TWELVE IMAGINARY LANDSCAPES

Oh time thy pyramids

– Jorge Luis Borges

Perfecting Thirst

Golden drench of sand, the backsweep and golden suck of the
tides of wind here in the flooded desert of our endless listening,
our endless attempts at incarnating water with the stone lintels of
mind and the small smirking mouth of a candle, a stubborn blind
icon. Trilobites of prayer puncture the walls like shrapnel. On the
night table I have closed the Book of Listening on waiting, since
the disappearance of the animals, for the beauty of their return.
The parched trees out there staggering toward their own mirage.
Something about who we've always been, between water and sand,
inoculated with the backsweep of light, endlessly recalcitrant.

There is, blindly, no after, so that if we were to say, *We were the
ones who were always here,* we would not be talking of time.

The After

A dark purple plunge, one that has the light set back in it, windless, where you could imagine running on empty, the one sticky fuel where the meteor had fallen, up the curved stairway into the library, as if you were in danger of finding yourself in a story by Kleist, hearing only the edge of what they were whispering, I would have thought perfection, how the future keeps slipping away like that but it pulls something out of you, the dogwood in bud again, as if there were something to believe in, as if there were a missed life for instance, this one not going quite as planned, and in the falling rain of its arced dust, figures emerge, haloed and blown, in their fizzing solders.

The Gleaner

Polypropylene, bone, moth-holed rusted tin, coiled pipe, spent fuel rods, bottles in aquamarine and smoky white, wasted light-year condensers, teeth, lesioned memory loops, an ivory chess piece, a bent key: the landfill closet of earth underfoot. The room I return to crammed to its ceiling of cloud with darkness in the lost city of found things, where sinks are rife with bullhead and pickerelweed.

Every day I go looking for it through the convoluted syntax of booby-trapped alleys and streets, smouldering grey oxides of rubbish heaps, derelict factories, warehouses, landfill mews.

Every night under the sfumato tower of dark I dream it. And what if one day I find it, at the end of a cobbled and walled cul-de-sac, through the quadratura battered wooden doors, past the ladders and stairs, abandoned dollies and trash cans, doors leading off into unseen interiors left or right, and without ringing the bell or leaving anything behind, I glide, moth-holed, through?

City of Heaven

Braided pyroclastic river of sky, the convulsions that light up the little I know, Monday 14 April, the antigravity city, igneous weightlessness, surplused from its roots in rock, rock that turbillions a high-tide apple tree's huge crown—something from your grandparents' grandparents' childhood—and its floating island. Whole parliaments are engorged and star chambered in the criss-cross current. Listen, an amphibious car breathing in the alleys. Only that, and the buzz of the evening's one last filament, a moth's Triassic light, levitating a world lifted up in tectonic stammer, unlawed by love. Whatever we do with our hearts in this jurisdiction is dangerous, a prayer of thyme on your fingertips, as when you lean over me and lift up your skirt, passing through the membrane of evening, the blood-brain barrier, rain barrier, the written chlorophyll of spine and spire, the death notice left on the night table.

Test

On waking this morning, the tear, the rent, the shattering blue in the smoke-grey sky, that first appeared a week ago ripping its way to the top of the tower, has splattered blue excitations through me, making me like one of the dreamed-up ones, blotted by brightness, while the smudged orange rubble fires on the horizon continue to mark the perimeter. And now the silencing device in my throat is giving me trouble. Spiked like a pollen grain and injected into the voice box, it swells there, pinning it shut from the inside. And naturally any writing devices—mechanical, electronic, chemical, genetic—are not permitted. The fuel marauders and suicide harrowers might be anywhere, and they live on information, of which we all must be starved. Splattering is everywhere. So I've hoarded old newspaper personals, fierce bracelets of tiny instruments, spangled areolae that direct my, needless to say, illegal research into emergent thought-vessels, this voiceless voice for instance, you might be hearing inside your head.

The Jetty

Hydrazine bramble branching over our heads along St. Lawrence Ditch, drenched with icicle fire, DNAed, backwarded, the viral supper that ate its children, the city finally owned by its outcasts, toxaphene thirst in the cells. Yanking the slave wrist upward and out, *Let's have a look at that.*

My life, composed of a series of stills, walks out to the jetty in one month of winter, like a bee whose shadow has stopped on the ground. I am already there, a meiosis of mind.

The Replicase

I'm cruising up against the splice, aspen-trembled anticipation in ghetto light, beyond the gene's jurisdiction, hot mist the colour of contusion latex. I know you, you're coronaviral pandemic, you've split open your hands, uncurbed mutagenics, and here I am, this listening with a single good auger, a single good protein trigger, bringing me out close to the empty shed, where all the roofs are ripening savannahs of wild grain, and here and there a stand of leafless yellowglow willow, the blue blank altar of sky, rushing me up against the edge of my body. I've come up from the landscape below the landscape, the breath below the breath, time beneath time, to kiss open its wager, its witness by water.

The Sea, the Valley and the Temple City

Clear creamy sky, fuchsia cloud traces over the nearly horizonless sea I wake to, the fine underslum of the godway, looking straight into the music where we cannot be, awaiting a ticket, the dive of the pliosaur armies, the moment the sea is higher than the valley, dropping away from the sea, the very waking edge of ocean, the rift valley a thousand feet below where the river is lazily thinking to itself. The ocean doesn't fall but the river spills into it so far away at the foot of the cliff the city spirals from. As if something were required of me. Torqued hive of fossil home dreamed from the shores of sleep, rising from the sea, older than sharks, older than shadow excavated by water, the nearly drowned tower, whose ghost language spills on me without mercy.

The Sect

Their pelts are anguish, a mere blur, animal with its windows open. I wake before the alarm, words piled on the night table, half-filled porcelain tumbler (a gift from the children), sun panning gold in the room, hum of air conditioner, dismantling the city of god. I had to go back there, criss-crossing the many pages, black wings of nights blinking by, returning a hundred million years to fetch the report from the night table, the sister planet, something like a flashback or false memory syndrome. (How do we know the truth?) Across the distances I'm begging you back —their bisphenol belief, minds lined up like the mantles of long extinguished naphtha lanterns.

The Survivor

I must have left the radio on. Tubes glow with the implied music of string theory, notelessly, forever, which only the cat can hear. I myself am waiting for an audible signal.

The sterile field over which gun-metal clouds are smelted has drowned the cathedral long ago, leaving only this chunk of flying buttress, a happy ruin you might say, because such as it is, it affords me a home, even if it's a bit creepy after the Great Collapse. People by the hundreds were hanged from the transepts and apses of where they used to pray.

But look over here on this side: a Bosch paradise with live pearls as if some father god had left toys for his children on Easter morning, had we but known what they symbolized.

At any rate, let me show you what I've managed to salvage: a red padlock, set of iron keys, three dice, saw blades for no known saw; night table with appointment card, clock, bed, stool, lamp, trilobite yo-yo, miraculous workbench with keyboard and vice, undetonated ordnance, auger, quills, this book.

Please ignore the sink of intestines under which St. Anthony seems to have left his mutant demons, cock-nosed and winged. They are harmless. Make yourself at home. Twirl a dial on the radio. I have stepped out but am sure to return.

The Welcoming Catastrophe

It's like looking back in time, our big sister planet looking back at us, with its seven small moons floating in the night sky, its faint reflected light polishing the long dark metals of the river. The volcano city breathes its fiery wraith-light up into the house of dark. We burn rock for blood, rhyolitic, obsidian, our gods are underground.

At Persephone's Gate where we met, I'll leave the silicate turbine of my heart, never looking back, driven by magma and ash.

When the Dead and the Living Change Places

Through the ceiling of chestnut trees, heavy with green fruit arching over the tram tracks, the manhole covers are open. They are open and the light falls through them. I hear the shower of light falling. Falling. It is late summer and the telephone lists and founders in the cobbled tramway. Foundering light also seeping from the book closed on the drowned night table where the tickets for the passage are misplaced. The unmade bed listing happily with the impression of the absent sleeper still in its arms. The radio, circa 1940, like what used to be called poetry, brings in the invisible voices, a little falling, opening, perturbation in time.

NIGHT MUSIC

The Before

In what remains there speaks a language
of the perishing of things. And what is perishable
has always been placed on the outside
of the circle of meaning, on the outside
of the eternal, but the hollow
bone is the soul of flight, as the vulture
tilting and rocking on a late September sea of wind vouchsafes.

I can do no more than this watching,
keep putting off the idea
of your not being here,
the interminable elusiveness of a life
now as paper-thin as your scalpelled skin,
the sutured list of operations
when one thing is becoming another
into which too much pain cannot be written.

"Dig that lady with the crazy hat"
on the sunny shores of Lake Superior,
snow on the prize-winning dahlias,
do you remember, Dad shouting to us not to panic,
the lee rail running, full of alarm,
the release in the dusk of a summer evening
from the prison of the neighbour's garden shed,
the yellowness of the evening grosbeaks
alight in the crabapple,
the September light pausing on the limit of summer,
passacaglia of light aloft in the pines
as if it were the experience of a single drop of darkness?

Half-Lives

How this surprised us. Because
death is an intransitive verb
like *to be*—
we think we're finally
about to understand
but we just don't, can't
know who the subject is,
for to you, who are no longer here,
neither am I
and I need to pretend
to an understanding
of this isotope of pain.

How you suffered the fission of
death scrawling through you
saying only
its easy part, the part
readable by us,
the wet ink of earth
blackening the spring drive home.
How, to produce it,
you ran your finger
along the sharp glass
of those last ten days
even jesting with nurses.

What has become
of then and now, now,
if ash is an isotope of bone
and faith of ash,
the thorium of breath
each atom of which
has an unpredictable moment
of decay?
There is
in the yard
a birch
with one remaining wing
of yellow leaves
as if it were
the half-life of happiness.

Last Note

Leaving now, the broken
bracken of the little letters
left in your blue daybook,
the sudden topography of it, the
turning away, and the still
being there, light
like stampeding horses
up through a flooded creek bed.

Unresectable, 11 May

Rain, in the season of the stink
of hawthorn, and pear,
crabapple blossoms—pink and
burgundy, so profuse, as if they thought
they were leaves. And now you,
again in hospital. Again the underwater
light. Your veins
sprouting plastic lines, small
purses of potassium and morphine
feeding the debt your body's racked up,
skin nearly the early colouring
of flowering dogwood bloom—
diverse lines: nasal line carrying
algal sludge from your stomach,
oxygen lines, kidney lines, as if
you were both diver and sea—

little mother, sleeping, delicately curled,
the empty palms of my hands might carry you.

How to Free the Past for the Future

One light, six truths; two names,
twelve months; one world, spilling
across this desk. An iris, five fingers;
the spun coins of twenty-four words.

What to do with all this wanting.
The long sear of caress that I will have
lived with so long, dropping its petals
(beyond count?) onto the surface of the water,
moaning with the body
wizened with its coming home
to forgone wisdom.

They say that time is dreamt
by the waking
to backfill the moment's mine
of the infinite,
they say the mind after death
begins to dream
and that the dream seems a life-
time long,
they say it is only time
that separates us,
its heartless beating
threaded shuttle weaving telling.

As If in an Henri Rousseau Painting

I'll pick up and carry all this sadness,
an archer retrieving arrows
on the boundary, their flights brilliant
with citrus and kohl, with Chinese
lantern, with cardinal, the cardinal
banking into the yard of
your adolescence, and a much later
year of my childhood, at the very
moment we paused there, right where
a door to the other world had been,
there it is again, after the slow,
measured, throat-breathing,
only occasionally
barbed on the in-breath,
how could you stop, mouth agape,
filling with interminable silence,
eyes still blue-grey bright,
seeing still what they saw
moments before, but more so—
stolen by it?

I am not prepared: the terrible,
tiny, helpless gesture of love,
the distancing, distancing
target of you.

Collection of Photographs

And so with this last and final and
irrevocable of parental deaths I come to the end
of not being thrown, not so much
into life, or even really into the living of it,
but into the abandonment of being in it,
holding on as long as possible
to the rituals of remembering, the loss
of my father for instance, consciously
constructed out of those of us left behind,
or the rituals of presence, photographing
flotsam on the scythe of beach
in the unfinished heat.

Everything has a space around it,
a kind of invisible purity
that's easily transgressed, every
moment, and each stays
remembered or not, mutilated
or not, as if now I were made of forgetting.

And I would want to be a friend of this thinking
that would put me beyond the pale
because that's the most interior moment,
the moment most intimate,
like the fold of family.

The Ruthie Tree

Flowering dogwood tracked you—
the flowering dogwood that would not flower
but spluttered each spring
a few meagre blossoms—

but inversely—we saw
the swelling purple-green buds, like fruit,
with the first flush of April heat together, poised
with the garden, and wondered how it would do,
transplanted as it had been,

and then the hospital, the small
sallow bloom, your skin
no longer worldly

as in the bar in Buffalo in the winter of '43,
the boys asking you
up to their room, and you, innocent, saying,
Sure, until Joan said, *Well, Ruthie...*—

the hard, tiny green flowers, and bracts
shuffling off their livids and their virids
leaving behind on one bank
the sallow and the bitter, enriching themselves
with what would become memory,
so that each day I looked at them
they were brighter and more supple
than the day before,
as each day you became weaker and more frail
until the tree blazed, fearsome, aerial
white, white

as milk, white as your hair
combed out by the nurses
at the end.

Belonging

After the service
driving past the house you were born and grew up in
and in which we spent my fifth year,
where through open windows
the cardinal's song drenched me,
the cardinal banked and veered into the yard
creasing and folding
the origami of time,
the house of the photo
after the wedding, before Dad went overseas,
the photo I have on the mantle of a different house,
the house the huge silver maple nearly toppled into
during the hurricane
and that looked so bereft afterward,
the house of the hemorrhage
and the sun porch in the shade,
the coal chute and cold cellar,
your father's prize-winning pigeons,
the house from which in a wood-panelled, nursery-school
station wagon I hated to leave you,
our house folded up in me we drive by
that now belongs to others.

Night Music

Tibetan bell orchestra of crickets
concentrating the night's darkness
into a liquor of late summer,
incessant tingsha stars.
I keep expecting the ringing
of your call.
You must be too busy
in reunion with the beloved dead.
What must the living be to you now?
We weep, remember, re-
imagine, forget, tell everything
our own way now, taking your
life into our own hands
lived, relived, unlived, as if
it were the sound of us thinking
or talking, the bells
whose soundings still try to hear you.

What Will Become

The storm shunting up the far shore for hours—
piling up basalt-black and bone-white clouds,
spitting lightning against the sunset—
would turn sometimes and without warning
like an angry god charge across the lake toward us
as if we were guilty of living,
hurling torn green hearts from the trees,
bullets of water—and silver maples
trying to run, would uproot themselves and fall
into smooth coffins of sand.
I would think of the thimble of the house—
windows trembling like terrified messengers—
and the wind sweeping my thoughts away,
the sun gone under, a torpedoed ship—
whole beaches would migrate
like refugees trying to escape the kingdom of war.

And I would grow tired, weary of the roar,
the continuous diatribe, the walking rocks, the corpses
of branches strewn at my feet, my heart
a buoy just above water, the broken shrouds of love.

How can I tell you how
you waved to the boy in the boat
adrift in your hallway so long ago
now that your hand is water, is cloud?

Well

How often we imagined something else
as an ending.
Now there are only hours left,
avalanches of pain past
plunged into pools
of morphine, and you are without
fear, your skin a geography
of purple continents, your eyes
unblinking, seeing
through everything.
I was there all morning
describing the clouds to you
from the song of the sky.
I shut up and followed
the tiny rill of your breath.
And I said, "Mom, can you see me?"
as I leaned over you. You
turned your head to me and
gave me a long, leisurely
blink, full of pleasure,
and then turned your head away.

The Lighthouse Dreamer

Sleep silos, sleep towers
at the noise of the open rivers
and the sea, that other place
where the complicated unrepentant
hungering words churn
their magma, their mafic dreams.
The lighthouse spits out its orientation
in a rhythmic, rucked and near-blind night
you would put your hands up over
your eyes to see—
how overcast, that sky
of scattered starlessness upon us,
putting your hands down at your sides.
Does the lens point
with its light, or core
the darkness as if exploring
the present were archaeology?
A ventriloquism of light,
metronome in the crashing water-and-stone thunder,
opulent geology burning
one photon of your juice at a time
as though there were three hundred and sixty degrees
of truth where only noise might know you.
How you mothered love into being there,
shone it out of darkness.

What Can Never Stop Having Been

All the histories are grass, the
vulnerable recursion of memory—
waxwing on miscanthus plume, splash
of night on its brow, streak
of cloud, narrow horizon.

Barely two generations:
mother, grandfather
and a few scattered stories
like seeds in snow.
It's March, and I'm hearing
the missing, seeing
this little blaze of bird: yellow on peach, droplet
of red, brighter than blood,
the white horses of my great-great-grandfather
like flying snow, the fortune
squandered.

My father's grandmother in the choir,
her husband I never knew
taking everything
but the apparatus of family,
leaving the tiny Chinese slippers
of the foot-bound princess,
or how you managed
twenty-one years without Dad,
the heart of your life.

There is no one
to tell it.
I am the discontinuous
the future rides on,
a family only waves of tenderness,
pain, fear or obligation,
regret or resentment
rippling through fields of
bleached grass heads standing above snow.

The Answer

Because you have answered,
of all possible answers,
with the one
you have been unbound with,
the dispersion of light
flying through the copse of catalpa
on the hill, your arm
propped up with tubes.

Because while you were answering
I sat in silence, in the mercy
of the light at the window,
the continuation and the changing
of weather, and everything
I am, and everything
I remember, is the house of everything
I've remembered and forgotten,
your arm propped up with clouds,
the trepidation and the confidence
in your hands, your hands
on the wheel, the raining down
of catalpa blooms as you drove
the Buick south to New York at fourteen,
Mother, she's doing just fine—
and this is your story—
your father turning to say so.
Or following one of the new Fairlane 500s
listening to your back-seat curled-up
ulcerous moans, the mercury of fear
rising. What will happen
is simple. You will get better
even in the United States with Canadian plates
miles from anywhere,
your arm propped up with continents of pain.

Because I have nothing to give
but these,
because if I could
and the impossible door that is a shadow.
Because something about the baby blue MGB,
the sun so hot before the rain,
your arm propped up with books
and all the maroon grandifloras.

Because of that answer,
because of the now open window
the crimson sun uses to set through,
I am still in that room,
the room of unfinishable stories.

Returning

Even when it's not called hope
our habit of looking to the future
when things might be different
is at the heart of every moment
and complicates our looking with time.

The dahlia imagining its fireworks—
and was it the silken-blown after-boom shapes,
smoke-trace of soul you were seeing in those last days?
I think when I looked at you then
I was looking with the weight of all my years
and I saw you as I had seen you
and that too was hope.

And I see you still
blooming in your dahlia garden,
the multiple branches sending their
pinwheel heads sailing over my mine,
a forest exploding with plum-coloured suns
where I could wander alone
and never be far from you.

Coda of Sighs

(after Anne Carson)

You forgot
the sighs of the ghosts of the
wind being
        felt up by pines
of silk slipping from skin, of
air over owl's wing,

        of the very last
out-breath
        taking you
beyond the pleasure of the dereliction
at the heart of that moment

of the letter
        sliding
out of its envelope
        unread

There is a moment
        before the sigh
where it is everywhere
        collecting itself
that the sigh says goodbye to
and scatters,
        the sigh
that is the soul, shimmering
on its edge
        with sharpness

Last Walk in the Garden

Your frailty made of insects and polished bird bone,
and though your feet hunt for footing
the bright hand-claps of your eyes enliven the near dusk,
the wind shapes you and the
chestnut chest of the nuthatch,
the water and the mineral in the rivers of rhizome
are listening for the last of the frost
and the first drop of sap at bud-tip.
Your husband stops his dreaming on the other side
as if he were Chuang Tzu, the clouds have been scrolls,
harps of the impossible, you have not seen him
for twenty-one years, and now—
after sleeplessness racked you
with its deserts and its vistas of icefields,
and your hand would reach out—
now to take each other in your arms
of ashes and earth.

LIKE THE SOUND OF A GRASS FIRE

Things Beckon

While at dinner in the open-air room
the most extraordinary thing happens.
People are standing and pointing and gasping.
We turn to look over our shoulders into the dark:
plumes of mango fire blistering the night.

The wet air is crushed
into periodic waves of hard noise, crashes and thumps
that strike our skins
with the geological loopiness of time
as if we were suddenly plunged, waiters and guests and all,
into the middle of the Cretaceous.

                      The volcano.
Its tip wrapped in the calyx of cloud since we arrived,
now decides on dazzle.

But, as if teasing us with destruction
not happening, it soon settles
into rhythms: only bits of fiery ash lighting up the sky,
wound of mouth,
and streams of red-gold coruscations.

We actually go to sleep.

In the morning when we walk onto the balcony
the whole mountain has vanished,
a burned-down candle,

and the eucalyptus below us releases
green darts of crimson-fronted parrots
into the silver impermeable light
that's after everything
at the beginning of everything.

Arrowhon Anniversary

The canoe glides out over the water, the submerged
reeds greenly bend in the current, clouds
slide over them reflected from the sky. The wind
strikes blue and white shards from it in gusts.
Gliding out over the sky, a cloud is a stone
made entirely of water and longing.
Reeds are lost forests.

Things are on different schedules:
the sun flowing over your bare shoulders;
kamikaze kingfishers plunging through
the crackled silence; bright darts
of hummingbirds, whizzing past us, turning
out the cluttered pockets of our hearts, scattering
their contents like sudden rain
and leaving, at the intersection of worlds,
weightless, the one true thing.

At the Pond

The water lily floats,
a gold crown of anthers
in its crimson bowl,
the colour of it deepening, pulling
the burst light into itself,
a cloud of blood in a green sky.

The long stalk shoots down into vanishing
canyons of liquid glass, blue backwashes of shadow.
Every day I follow this path down
to try to find where the heart begins,
the shiny ribbon in the dark tangling
among the long ganglia of leaf stalks
so that I lose my way.

And every day for three days
it unfolds itself
in the eye of the sun,
but on the third day it forgets to open
as if it had drunk all the light
it could bear, and now
has enough fuel to dream forever.

Finally, one morning, it has vanished completely
returning to Atlantis, a temple's handbell.

Early Spring Night by the Lake

Stars, burrs of light
caught in the dark stuff of sky,
near-words in the throat; the lake,
under the bone needle of moon
sewn with aluminum threads,
voodoos its many lives. I am
on the shore of them, effigied,
unmercied, stitched to the night's sleeve.

From still black branches
new leaves hang, tiny wet green hands
or the lungs of songbirds, trails
of fireflies like scars.

Himalaya

Let the burnished gauze of sky-smoke billow,
unfurl over barren rock face, ragged edge of storm
memory, setting sun torn, you are down on your luck
among the pyres, the squalls of light, the broken
pinions of lungs, the jewelry
of all the little ankle bones.
Let the rock be rock and the lichen lichen,
orange and green and grey
where lammergeiers turn wind to wings, marrow
to the instant zoom of vision, let
the fires of the mind leap up
and burn nothing down.

Every Part of You Has a Secret Language

It is not like anything, vivids, lurids, smoke, some truth
imitating the shiver of music, the river that empties itself
into what we call, for want of a better word,
the mind, the cascading of autumn dogwood leaves
into the pond in a gust of wind, fingertips
rilling down skin, every object a time gate.

In Jerusalem you can walk down into history,
the savage, yearning, human dust that, in the name
of gods, eats us, and which, though when mixed with light,
heated and bent, in October 1999, we saw sprout
spathes and pods and saguaros in the shimmer and glow
of pigmented—ferric, xanthic, azuritic—glass
that made of the Tower of David,
the feeling of someone walking into an orchard in spring.

It might be the hollowed bones of the thinking
of the planet, the birdsong on the periphery
of the film's soundtrack, unobtrusively,
in the cloud forest, the intermittent
thumping of the volcano hidden in the mist
when the heart is a hummingbird, thrumming
through the blue of your hand, or the room
where we make love (your body like water, like myrrh, like
the sound of a grass fire, or two girls whispering before dance class)
with, this morning, it's organza and charmeuse sunlight.

Whatever it is—this thing, before which words stumble,
that happens to us, this us—it's not possible
to be alive in it, and not have everything.

Nagarjuna and the Grackle

Spit of black fuel flying through the boson field of equinox,
its tar-sand mirrors, its shiny purple smoke
opening the dictionary of wings at the word
keelhauled, at the word *cranked*, its twenty-four carat eye
clocked at eternal half-life, the clashing sword, bolt-action, sprung brass-
against-glass, tocsin-voiced, rummaging, desperate, in a drawer of seed.
For what?

On the Skyline

Rain needles draw their fine thread
through the blown silk of white, pearl grey,
charcoal crepe cloud, abrupt blue,
sudden sun sequin dazzle,
flickering wells of shadow
steep sudden plunges in temperature,
the high furling swell of the stone sea of these mountains
over which the scrawl of cloud shadow drifts
and vanishes, drifts and vanishes.
                              I am overtaken by things
for whom I don't exist.

Residual Messages

What if you woke in a room you seemed
not to know, as if
floors, walls and ceilings,
were shallow water, spoked with light,
someone's careless conversation churning the water wheel
of the minutes, liquid anxiety
like hummingbird plumage, and the objects that found you right away,
or shortly after, could hear the shimmer of darters,
glissando of grass, the sky
torn blue at the seams?
They'd look through motives like glass, the thrill of blue everywhere,
or the long list of dos and don'ts.
What if you were a sifting of
residual messages, light searing the retinal sea floor?

The Clearing

The rain's thin legs walking to the ends of the earth
as if time itself could carry meaning,
the house floating over the swollen river
insouciant as a water lily,
a Japanese beetle
looks in through a window with glistening eye.
Scattering ashes of the dead
makes a great wing in the grey air
which this little arc of thought mimics:
our life held in suspension.
I have to open the door, but it keeps getting
smaller, a secret
passage, narrow as thirst
that one movement of the arm
just under the eyelid of sleep might
waken the door handle's carapace,
a flower head gone to seed.
The white sleeves of rotted birch, akimbo
on the forest floor, light
exploding in the clearing.

The Counter-Tree

Burnished anthracite of sky
and a single tree in negative—
a noiseless white fracture,
and upward sprung

and motionless lightning
as if the winter storm
had swept time away,
shocked memory
into reverse

and x-rayed something
caught in the act:
its held breath,
its halide laughter
a near infrared verb
as if
a thing could be known
only by its shadow,
the one it carries lightly
under its tongue.

Two Time

The endless conversation:
crickets and water falling on rock
shape the night, as a bowl
shapes space, or language might
an unfound thought.
First a woman's voice, then
a car engine, then a flood
of wind in the Jack pine, a stagger
in the mind, fall into this pond
disturbing its surface momentarily, only
to be absorbed, forgotten even.
For a moment I think:
a narrative, little instances of time.
But it's not the sequence, it's the difference
between the aural luminosity of cricket water
and the hurt in the voice.
It's the voice of water, spiked,
until the next oblivion.

Were You to Walk

through this wood
astringent ghosts of moonlight
in the stands of pine, the smallest
of mercies, drawing their night's
dark out, so dense it could be
the memory at the root of a star
older than the insect musicians
that *da capo* their brittle codas here
thin as a keyhole—(that portal
to everything we can lay claim to)
a self dusted with bone light.

Three Quotations

1

A thought arises like a single stemmed water iris
as blue as blue as
a gasp of sky out beyond the edge of the pond.

Over wet stones an orange crowned ovenbird hops.

There is no history here, merely one thought
over another, ply on ply. I am another.

Water slips over water, over stone,
heat ripples air over rock.

Sun's caught in the red-tail's ruddering,
a vole's heart bursts.

How do we know anything?

...everything was fading before our eyes, and... many of the loveliest of colours had already disappeared, or existed only where no one saw them...

2

The little house I was born into after the war: one of those things
over which others slip, wind or cloud or constellations,
and through which how many others have since come and gone?

These words: *spooked, claimed,* a little swirl, scilla
of violence, whose reach-spirals squander, inhale.
How about *tuned*? How a life tries to align itself
with things that seem so truculent, intransigent,
specular or spectacular.

OK, let's put one word in front of another.
And keep going, splintered tenderness, the whole tower
going down like one of its own elevators.
And this falling continuing inside me.

But what are you doing here then, Ma'am?
She wanted to explain that that's what her life was like,
but not knowing what she meant by "that's what it's like" or
"her life" she didn't answer.

The phalaenopsis, after months in bloom, one morning offers
instead of its white waxen flowers,
tiny crumpled handkerchiefs of parting.

None of us can be inward enough. Inward enough
to even know the name of this threshold. Delible as dust.

We gather up our things and glance at the door.
We glance back at the TV repeating its images
of lost astonishment we keep refusing to understand,
stuttering as if time had become stuck,
a stylus in a gouged record.

3

Sooty birds, juncos, chickadees, whose flight
careens across the edge of generations
of sorrow in the persistent cinerary snow
in the dusk, to each other appear
as people, but to us, as in an underworld,
have forgotten how to speak,
not as history, and it's really not possible
all those individual joys, juices, *little box*
of seashells, the miniature barrel organ, the globe-shaped
paperweights with wonderful marine flowers swaying
inside their glassy spheres, the model ship, the kisses
that entered the depths of the lovers
and transformed them, husbands
blasted into other worlds, women
whose tongues had been torn out.
There are some things we will never know,
or not know until it's too late, some
we don't want to know
because it places us on the wrong side of things.

On Upper Paradise Road, in the Catholic church
where I took my first of only two communions,
I being an unbelieving Protestant,
there were pictures of hearts with what I understood to be wings.

Here in the aftermath of history, snow is light
in plumed seed heads, in its continual falling,
mica, glinting like voices, and the cardinal
at the feeder is a heart with wings,
or maybe it's really flames.

The Book That Can Be Read from Its Shelf

This book can be read from its shelf,
from the side that your particular tongue would read from
and by people of all languages and is laid out in "tongues"
and is meant to certify the actual existence
of all that is described on this day,
that is, to certify the birth of the book:

human body (skinless); the first
third of the Milky Way; hand (extended);
map (in every scope of the word)
and under constant discussion.

In every map you will find the next map.

They left us a giant machine in the desert.
The machine will be turned back on.
The clock is ticking.

Orion is on the earth in the form of pyramids
instead of stars. Take a map of the human body
and lay it on top of Orion. Focussing on Orion's belt
you may begin to see the lamp stand, or ark,
the black space that works with the stars.
They are trying to get you to see that the woman
is looking in the direction of the rising sun
with the river as the ground beneath her feet.

I have sent copies of the book around the world;
some locations will hide the copies that were sent to them
as instructed, and it will bleed across the borders.
The book will be two-sided as the desert:
one side shall represent the day and other the night;
one side shall represent the living who are in the day
and the other shall represent the dead who are in the night.

There shall be six languages coming into one side of the book
and six languages into the other.
The section of Diagrams and Figures shall be the seventh section.
Seven: honouring the number of towers,
continents, angels, hills, days, churches, powers,
knowledges, thunders, eyes, as well as the Seven Trumpets,
and you shall find the rest.
All things possible will be covered within the walls of these pages
but what you shall see in the desert when the clock is full.

I have been to so many places
I think I'll stop now and write this book.
Set aside (30) minutes to assemble it.

The Last Word, A Sharawadji

> *…true conversation is a pure play of words.*
> – Roberto Calasso

I wouldn't know where to begin, even if
I were to begin at the most commonsensical of places,
the thread of an uncertain conversation,
sporadic, suddenly tethered like a sky
by lightning to the distant tumid twist of shore.

I can say, *He bit into it as if it were an apple, taking a large bite,*
almost half the heart, that room
with the scattered signature of stars,
scattered archipelagos after the storm I wake to
and don't know, one of the hungry ghosts.

But I fail to understand them; they've come thousands of miles
to see something they would never be able to see
and when you show it to them they turn away,
the mothers carrying their dead children
out of the cities of fire in suitcases,
the plane slipping into the envelope of the tower,
the light sweeping across the room like a golden shower,
using up every dram of memory
someone goes into the jungle, someone
opens a book, someone *looks into a mirror*
only to never return.

What would they say
if they knew we were *passing each other*
in streets smeared with neon, fugues of stars,
scattered memory light
of the lost world after rain, *unrepeatably*?

PREVIEWS

...while we sleep here,
we are awake elsewhere...

– Jorge Luis Borges

Animal Light

This morning I found myself feeling strangely disoriented as if I'd crossed a boundary I hadn't known was there. The warrant for the arrest lay on the night table among the word-bloom traffic that had once belonged to someone by the name of Mayröcker. So I went down again to the church ruin, cathedral ruin, its psychopharmacological rain, field of wounded error and splinter quires, long since the extinctions.

What was I doing? I should have been at home watching the news, but I was flooded there unable to lacerate it, quilled to its backbone just beneath the membrane of breath, my hands aflame in the last oxygen, incapable of measuring its forgetfulness, its whispering haywire hunger, its animal light.

Apocrypha

Her name was a small sculpted flute sound and she took it upon herself to move among things little by little in the ransacked light. Look how young! And now to be shaking hands with angels.

I am walking down to the river there, carrying a burden of ash, the beauty of all the lost arguments, the car abandoned by the river, its gills glistening. Plague flags flying. The queen having none of it. You too would resist.

I can see now how the war takes its toll from each of them right here at the bridge. Embarking, disembarkation. Another life. No. It's just this one, the one she can imagine here and now, and that's what it is, all of it, and she takes it.

Hospital of the Dark

Holding itself against the current of its dissolution, so that it flickers like a candle or a lamp's bad connection—curtains billowing, subsiding, billowing. And reaching into the room, a sound like a surveillance beacon.

Something snaps on; I am awake, light sluicing down through the ganglion of an ancient apple tree, a high tide of barley flooding to its glottal drip-line. The farm house a thirst of wood up the hill, the sky a kind of sky machine generating labial pinks, dissolutions of graphite, waves of things coming at me, and the susurration of the river to my right.

At night, in the room I'm to sleep in, there is lightning, lightning and no thunder holding itself against the current in longhand. Oh the ceiling of stars, constellations never before seen, or seen only once in childhood, or in a movie in childhood, or a dream in childhood, or a story read to you in childhood. And then the voice you are hearing inside your head wobbles, gutters out.

Someone wakes up, marrow-chilled, in a field of stones. Up the hill, the ruin of a house, a well, run dry with memory.

In the Zone

Millions of years ago in the future, radium moonlight, the one kiss carried into an attic of rain, is a cloudburst of brain-stored fireflies, a drizzling glow in the bones. Here people are holding themselves together against feral atmospheres with psychotropic weather. I seem to recognize things, a sadness as if held down by stones, but the closer I look the more they slip from recognition. The river I once walked along, flowing now the other way, undetectably contaminated; palms, carboniferous cycads; the sign for caution, an empty glass; the semiconductor, "D," spelled backwards. Time's begun to think of itself as a slip knot, the well of the kiss, its half-life, its scorched fingerprint, annealing us into the face of the earth.

A Momentary History of Time, *or,* The Sheer

Esse est percipi
– George Berkeley

It is not memory, the new things having thrown off their inadvertent poisons, the open cadmium window, the giant cycad forest stilled after stormlight's darkened moment. The once. The again. Sequenceless. You. The same. One hundred million years. *Undo the cations on the owl wing voice,* you'd said, standing at the top of the stairs, naked but for the green necklace in its sheer brocade, and you weren't fooling, or falling. And the one she sang the book to, who, without understanding, would carry it across, under Babel, under bone highway, through the mantle, the burning furniture of the world. Trichloroethylene's eye that would be water. This is that moment. Proleptic. That the thirst that cannot be quenched might still be perfected.

Poisoned

Broken into and lost across the lightgrid, holed up in the century after the first flowering plants, the ruined chimneys, rubbled roads having long ago exhausted the nutation of the carbon zone, the member states' slab suction under the spell of the luminous night streaming scimitared moons, I'm waist deep in gragger grass, the bar code burning on my shoulder just beneath the awareness threshold, the forest up ahead filled with night fog, shadows a writing on the greensilver I've forgotten how to read, each leaf a lens. If only my map were still alive. The girl's poisoned lipstick—I would not normally have said anything. So I follow the hoops of storm cells windmilling on the rise, and from there down below in the valley to my right, rising on stilts in the middle of the river, the lacrimal, ethmoid, parietal house, about to fold up and dive like a pelican into the river's memory's slow toluene.

Portrait

The night is a liquid dark, reeds lay themselves in silver lines down on its black surface, the slowly returning abundance of earth, though a stump shines like the burning of the towers of a ruined city and, like dragonflies, fuel-less helicopters are arrayed on the jetty.

There is a fear someone may enter the room. Inside, a man, someone unknown, whose face is a stop-frame film of emotion: just holding back tears, smiling hopefully through them, rinse of panic, hint of an attempt to muster resolve, to lay itself down on what is held dear, and what is still held at a distance. And whatever it is returning that is looking at him says, I am not a woman, I am a language become soul arrayed in splinters of thirst.

Something to Remember the World By

The hotel by the sea had simply vanished, its long alfresco bar that you stepped down from the boardwalk into included, and been replaced by a row of old unpainted boarded-up storefronts. How could this be? My luggage, my wife, my perfect sense of place and time, gone. It's always the same: it's midnight or three a.m. and the polished peephole of the moon is bright. The white heat of the pain in my head flashing on and off like a buzzer of light. I get the feeling I need to turn around and look behind me, the always important step of coming back, as if there might be recognition.

Recognition? Something to remember the world by. The dazzling land as if lit from below. I lie there in the hotel room, the tickets on the night table, the ceiling fan slowly slicing the currents of lamplight, opening this thought like a book, somebody's name on the tip of my tongue.

Among the Harvested

Truth is peregrine, each life a vector in the backward surge of time. I say this not just because of the events of the past few days; we know perfectly well everything ends. Truth is peregrine, picking its way among ruins, rubble, halocarbons and hatreds, spent shell casings and syringes, the old technologies, technologies of gathering and gunning down, death-pit technologies, and *ting ting*, hiding its name in dusty police files, perhaps coded, when for instance the word *work* spoken over the radio meant *kill:* "Everyone should work more carefully." But truth can't even be caught in this subtle manner. It flies through your net, the net of your need, as if it were a mere phantasm. I too dreamed of the knock on the door. It was someone else's door, a door in a pulverized landscape, where I could see neither people nor animals.

The Invasion

The nearly breathing ships, lights gilling, hovering, scrying for us, the hidden, under the houses' bamboo floors by the edge of the lake, the deep black translucence of its calmness magnified by terror closing our throats, the drain of the moon on the lake's floor suddenly opening.

Where was my son? I was feeling permeable to light, but might be detected by the breath I held spiking in my hand, the sudden downpour of an idea. Keep your mind cloudless I'd told myself.

Someone was standing, dishevelled, shouting at the ground, a cedar waxwing wanted to burst through a picture window, the apple tree pulling its apples out by their stems. Each might be him, feigning a physical presence.

All this happens just as their ploughs, unfolding, enter what's left of the lake, the water turning over the leaves of its volumes of moonlight written completely in the dark.

The Last

Up from the overmeasured but strewn streets, not knowing what to say, not knowing whose life to enter after the burning of the languages, regicides of pollen long ago catasterized, the cut-by-flying-glass of trying to recall you.

Everything we've known's been altered or lost—such human-headed obstinance. However we might have turned, left, right and left again, we never changed direction, and however often the idea of stopping came into our heads—because in the idea of stopping may be the idea of dying—we never stopped, but here things stand anyway. Only marksmanship's saved my ass.

So it's here we've gone back, alas foolishly, and against the edicts, as if through the door of a temple sleep, and name fragments washed up on the shore of it, and one of them chose each of us, names we'd never before heard and now heard for the first time, backwashing through shingle.

We are maculate with them, jubilant with the polluted nucleotide pools, the remnant greens the corporate armies've threshed; with the blaze of final number, the hunger made of chlorophyll wings and the fine poison spines of lionfish, we are last.

Then

The night screamers, their tellurium-sequenced mandate, their machetes' minds' lost wax, opprobrium without appeal, sectioning the streets.

Then the basement labs synthesizing priceless exquisite squalls of rust on iron, heaven crushed into potable gutters, glittering racemes.

Then the slow inevitable blossom effect with evening triggers and layers of titanium cloud shearing away right to the bone, automobile awnings and tasselled carcasses.

Then a trout-skinned, rain-skinned figure pulling each word out of its cell envelope, furan-fangled, so that it might burst into flame. Grit. Gristle. Blushed and blemished, famished and finished, the words that broke their teeth on me and spat me out.

Time Runner

In the lightfold of dataplume, the careening, warping, flaring slave kenosis, the ministries of rust and bone, acetylene emblazoned trees as if from some autumnal northern hemisphere of an old earth, the mind is a burst of darkness, plangent, like a kiss, hiding the forgotten thing, until it glances suddenly back, and you glimpse the other life that lived it and is yet to live it, a time runner, volcanoed out, the stranger in the bathroom of the unbuilt house, the tearing through the head-high weeds and blackened, burnt-down alphabet of trees, clinkers embedding, itching into skin, sky a thumping burst of smudged red glow on grey cloud. Tonight I dream my arms curve out like wings and I fly over the silver water of the lake and the silver rock of the shore. Freedom is what has been done to you, divided by itself, decayed shunt of the story of something sheared along the fiery fractal of your pain, an interior of an interior of words.

Notes

Many of the poems in Part I, Twelve Imaginary Landscapes, and Part IV, Previews, began as experiments in ekphrasis, reading some of the paintings of Jacek Yerka (whose haunted landscapes displace evolutionary time and the laws of physics, and allow elements of Bruegel, Van Eyk and Magritte to mingle), but mutated rather quickly away from translations of works of art.

The Jetty
The image of the bee's shadow stopped on the ground is lifted from Borges' ficcione, "The Secret Miracle" (translated by Harriet de Onis in *Labyrinths*, New Directions).

The Sect
The black wings that blink by are what happens to our perception of time on first lift off in Wells' time machine.

When the Living and the Dead Exchange Places
The title is a line from Tomas Tranströmer (translated by Robin Fulton in *New Collected Poems*, New Directions).

What Can Never Stop Having Been
The title is from a phrase from Merleau-Ponty ("a present that can never stop having been").

Every part of you has a secret language
The title comes from Rumi's poem "Joy from Sudden Disappointment" (translated by Coleman Barks in *The Essential Rumi*, Harper Collins).

   The reference to glass: Dale Chihiuly's show in the Tower of David Museum in 2000 (http://www.chihuly.com/jerusalem/jerusalem.html).

Three Quotations
   1. From *Austerlitz*, by W.G. Sebald (translated by Anthea Bell, Random House.
   2. From *Soulstorm*, by Clarice Lispector (translated by Alexis Levitin, New Directions.
   3. From *Austerlitz*, by W.G.Sebald (as above).

The Book That Can Be Read from Its Shelf
The phrases that constitute this piece were found in a now lost manuscript source.

The Last Word, A Sharawadji
The word *Sharawadji* was first used by Sir William Temple in *Upon the Gardens of Epicurus* (1685) to describe the effects of the "oriental style" in which "beauty shall be great, and strike the eye, but without any order or disposition of the parts that shall be commonly or easily observed."

Augoyard and Torgue (in *À l'écoute de l'environment. Répertoire des effets sonores,*" from *The Book of Music and Nature*, edited by David Rothenbuerg and Marta Ulvaeus, Wesleyan University Press) have written that a *sharawadji effect* "takes one by surprise and will carry the listener elsewhere, beyond strict representation—out of context."

Claude Schryer, who has picked the term up for his electroacoustic soundscape compostional practice says that searching for this effect "is essentially a state of awareness" ("The Sharawadji Effect," also from *The Book of Music and Nature*).

The italicized phrases were overheard in Tobias Schneebaum's *Secret Places: My Life in New York and New* Guinea (University of Wisconsin Press), and Robert Calasso's *Literature and the Gods* (translated by Tim Parks, Random House).

Animal Light
Friederike Mayröcker: see especially *brutt, or The Sighing Gardens* (translated by Roslyn Theobald, Northwestern University Press).

In the Zone
The Zone is the restricted area around the site of a strange occurrence in Andrej Tarkovsky's film *Stalker,* and which presages its use for the "no-go" area around Chernobyl.

A Momentary History of Time, or, The Sheer
The phrase "thirst…might still be perfected" takes up the epigraph from Galway Kinnell's book *Imperfect Thirst* (Houghton Mifflin Harcourt): "If your eyes are not deceived by the mirage / Do not be proud of the sharpness of your understanding; / It may be your freedom from this optical illusion / Is due to the imperfectness of your thirst," attributed to the Persian philosopher, Suhrawardi.

Among the Harvested
"Everyone should work more carefully" was code used on Rawandan radio when coordinating genocidal attacks.

Ting ting is Ugandan slang for prepubescent girls used as slaves.

Acknowledgements

My sincere thanks to the editors of *Rampike, Descant, The Antigonish Review, Prairie Fire* and *Canadian Literature* for including some of the poems (sometimes in slightly different form) from the developing manuscript of this book in their venues.

I'd like to thank Di Brandt and Karl Jirgens for their kind support. And Beth; it was great coming close with the last one. Thanks also to Tim Lilburn and Don Domanski.

To Loris for continued conversations, and to Ed for his supportive comments on this work and all the others, and for coming back to find the balls still in the air.

Thanks, too, to Adrian, Kyra and Sean for listening.

It's often fun but almost always a challenge to bring out an actual book. The folks at Brick do this with panache, and I thank them all heartily. Don McKay, my editor, pulled rabbits out of hats when we needed solutions. Thanks (once again) for your magic skills. Thanks to Alayna for her insightful precision and care, to Alan for his fine design and to Kitty for, well, being Kitty.

And to Charlene, I say, *the raft of our love.*

Biographical Note

Brian Henderson is the author of nine previous collections of poetry, the most recent of which, *Nerve Language* (Pedlar Press, 2007), was a finalist for the Governor General's Award. He holds a PhD in Canadian Literature and is the director of Wilfrid Laurier University Press. He began his publishing career co-editing the literary journal *Rune* in the 1970s, and then worked in college publishing in various roles from editorial assistant to publisher with Harcourt Brace, McGraw Hill, Copp Clark, Oxford University Press, Harper Collins and Addison Wesley. He has taught at York University and in the Ryerson publishing program and has served as president of the Association of Canadian University Presses, and Treasurer for the Association of Canadian Publishers.